Applying Six Sigma Tools to Human Resources: Case Studies and Scenarios

INTRODUCTION

"I am so busy. I have to interview 75 people for 15 jobs in 3 different plants in 10 days" said Trish Brown the Corporate Human Resources (HR) VP for a large international $1B manufacturing company

"Why not just hire some help?" I asked.

"I did.", Trish said. "I had to fire 3 contract workers in the past 2 months as well as 2 placement firms; all for not following my instructions."

She sighed, obviously frustrated. "No one listens and follows directions anymore. You can't hire good people!!"

My first thoughts as a Lean Six Sigma Master Black Belt extraordinaire (if I do say so my own self) were, You had to fire 5 different people in 2 months for not listening and following your instructions and you think you can't find good PEOPLE?

Let that sink in for a second.

If you keep having to let people go for not following your instructions, don't you think that maybe, just maybe, the fault is NOT them?

Ever think that it is your instructions are at fault?

A $500M family owned business in the middle of nowhere Ohio, is a Tier 1 supplier to the major auto makers. So they sent parts directly to GM, Ford and Chrysler.

For the past several months they have been bleeding money due to a quality problem on one of their parts. The fall out or defect rate is over 25%. As a result they have to work overtime and make many more parts to meet demand. The parts are shipped by air so as not to shut down their customers manufacturing lines, which would incur a hefty fine as a result of their contractual agreement. They even have had to have a helicopter land on their property, hand carry boxes out to it, and fly it directly to the parking lot of a GM plant in Detroit.

They have brought in several technical experts to look at a welding machine to see what could be the problem on why the machine is making so many bad parts.

All the while, they never realized it was an HR problem that could be easily fixed.

WHAT IS HUMAN RESOURCES (HR)

"They add no value"

"Why do we have them around?"

"They are so noisy. They know everyone's salary, their performance appraisals, who has made complaints against whom….."

"I always worry when I have to deal with HR"

Those are things you normally hear in any large corporation about the HR department.

In many ways all are valid questions. Why DO companies have them around? What is their contribution to an outfit?

Do they add value?

In the traditional Lean definition of "value" the answer is "no".

Lean Manufacturing, or Lean Processing, is a term used to describe a highly efficient process where waste has conscientiously been eliminated or attempted to be eliminated.

It is based on the Toyota Manufacturing process which is considered world class in their manufacturing of cars.

The name was given by Dr. James Womack. Dr. Womack was a MIT professor who spent 5 years looking at manufacturers around the world to report who and what "worked" the best.

In 1990 he wrote "The Machine that Changed the World" in which he described Toyota's method of manufacturing and dubbed it "Lean" as in very lean, little fat, little waste, etc.

Anyway.

In Lean thinking something is of Value if it:

"Changes the form or function of a service or product in a way that a customer is willing to pay for it."

The key words here are customer is willing to pay for it.

What this boils down to is that work done by factory assembly workers, call takers who take orders that start a process, cable installers, repairmen, and other type of work are all examples of value added activities.

When customers pay for products and services they are in actuality paying for the work done by these people.

Managers, supervisors, quality inspectors, even CEO's are all NON-value added. No customer wants or is willing to pay for someone to watch over, check or supervise someone else DOING real work.

And YES, HR would be considered non-value work as well.

In that sense HR does not add value.

But does that mean HR is not needed?

Could any company of over say 50 people just fire their HR staff and tread along merrily making money?

I doubt it.

Do managers have time to go out and find new employees, interview them, arrange their on site visit schedules, come up with compensation packages that are competitive, on top of a slew of other time-consuming things?

No they don't.

Do CEO's want to get involved with the training plans and methods of every new or advancing employee in their companies to insure all the right people are in the right jobs doing the right things so they can advance and improve the company?

No they don't.

And what about all the worker conflicts? Sexual and racial discrimination charges or potential law suits?

Who will take care of those things?

You guessed it—HR.

A few but not totally exhaustive list of items HR takes care of in any large corporate enterprise are:

-finding and interviewing new employees

-onboarding new employees.

-handling retirement plans.

- researching competitive compensation plans.
- analyzing various health care and benefits packages.
- coming up with overtime policies.
- coming up with work place attire policies.
- dealing with union contracts and issues.
- dealing with employee complaints.
- handling disagreements between employees.
- handling disagreements between employees and management.
- annual appraisal reviews.
- analyzing attrition rates.
- conducting exit interviews.
- often times public relations communications.
- often times involved in training.

…you get the picture.

So while by a strict Lean definition, HR is non-value add (like most salaried positions, including Six Sigma Master Black Belt-the horror!) that does not mean it is not NECESSARY.

HR is necessary for every company that has two or more people.

So if HR is necessary and you have to have it around, shouldn't you at least make sure this non-value added activity is performed as efficient as it possibly can be?

And that is where Six Sigma fits in.

WHAT IS SIX SIGMA?

Six Sigma is a problem solving method. It was created by Motorola in the late 1980's or so. It pools together a lot of problem solving techniques from statistics, group/team building, etc. brings them all together under one roof so to speak so that engineers, manufacturers, and other people in corporate America can get to the root cause of problems in industry and eliminate them.

Its power comes in the common nomenclature, a roadmap of steps to go from problem definition to solution in a way everyone onboard can follow along. The purpose being that nothing is overlooked, no conclusion unwarranted, no assumptions go unchallenged, etc.

While its origin and application is most appropriate in manufacturing of goods, more and more Six Sigma tools are being used in other areas such as: finance and accounting, telecommunications, banking, medical billing, and other transactional areas of businesses.

It follows a problem solving format of: DMAIC. This stands for:

D-Define

M-Measure

A-Analyze

I-Improve

C-Control

What that means is that a group of people working in concert usually attack a given problem by

-**Defining** what the problem actually is, and doing so in as quantifiable form as possible. Making the problem specific and measurable is key in this step.

-**Measuring** just how bad the problem is, and how it compares to past performance, the competition or some other standard.

-**Analyzing** various data about the problem to determine what are the important features. This attempts to find the key input variables that effect the problem and attack those specific inputs.

- **Improve** involves making the key inputs do what you want them to do in order to make the final result correct. This is usually where the actually solution is discovered for the original problem

- **Control** is all about measuring, monitoring, and yes controlling the key input variables so that the problem you just solved stays solved forever and ever.

In the U.S. it is said about 60% of US companies in the Fortune 500 use this Six Sigma DMAIC process somewhere in their company to solve problems of a variety of natures

HOW DOES SIX SIGMA APPLY TO HUMAN RESOURCES?

That summary of Six Sigma was all well and good, but what pray tell does that have to do with HR?

Well consider this, Human Resource professionals provide and deliver a service to their customers. Their customers in most cases are the companies for whom they work.

Anything that involves a process that deliver a service or product to a customer that is looking to improve upon said service or product, is an area that could use Six Sigma methods.

Unless there is an organization or field that can deliver 100% quality and accuracy, 100% of the time then there is a place for process improvement efforts like Lean, Theory of Constraints, Shainin problem solving and yes, Six Sigma.

Over the course of my 16 year career in Six Sigma I have happened to come upon several applications of Six Sigma in the HR realm.

I will go over several in the following pages. I've taken the liberty to change the names and places to protect the innocent and guilty of course so no one need be called out or embarrassed by the recognition of their name and place of work.

I can be very discrete like that.

Consider a few of these cases and scenarios:

CASE STUDY 1: YOU LIVE WHERE?

MAN VS DISTANCE

"Every place is walking distance if

if you have the time"

Stephen Wright

A company that performed some very technical manufacturing operations for the aerospace industry was having a problem with employees leaving. And by leaving I mean just up and quitting never to return.

More often than not with no explanation.

Historically this company had only a 15-18% attrition rate. That was in line with a general manufacturing attrition rate of 15% for their region; generally accepted as the norm.

Following a couple of years of a lot of hiring activity due to increase work volume, the attrition rate suddenly jumped to 31%.

This was well outside what one would have expected given an average of 15-18% each year.

In fact the odds of that happening by chance alone were well less than 2.5%. (This was calculated using the Six Sigma Tools of Process Capability, Z-scores and the Normal Distribution)

Clearly something was amiss.

Traditionally when it comes to attrition problems, HR personnel use Exit Interviews as a tool to gather data to try to get at the root cause of why people are leaving. While this idea indeed has a lot of merit, there are no Exit Interviews when employees quit unannounced, or just don't return.

In an hourly manufacturing environment where the work can be very laborious, difficult, boring, etc. it is not that uncommon for employees to do just that. Quit and never return leaving behind little clue as to why.

This was a non-union environment that had experienced steady growth over the years. Originally founded by two good friends in the late 1970's, it had gone from a lonely operation in one man's garage to having over 300 people and over 30 sophisticated cutting machines (CNCs) under one roof.

In this particular instance the company had data for the past 2 yrs. for about 100 employees that they had recently hired to meet their work uptick.

Of these 100 that were hired, 32 had quit in that same 2 yr. period.

In order to analyze this problem then, they would have to just use the data they had available to see if that revealed anything of importance.

A simple discrete data hypothesis test (2 proportion test) with:

-"hourly vs. salary".

-"1st vs. 2nd" shift.

-male vs. female.

-college educated vs. non-college educated.

 as the attributes to analyze, showed no statistically significant difference between any of these variables. (Using Six Sigma Tools of Hypothesis testing)

HOWEVER

A Logistic Regression analysis was performed using: "Gender", "prior years of manufacturing experience", and "commute distance" was conducted.

Note: in traditional regression analysis one is looking for a correlation between some "x" or independent variable and some "y" or dependent variable.

The goal being, to be able to predict the "y" response, given a specific "x" value.

For instance what will the humidity be outside (our "y" in this example) given the temperature (our "x'). That is humidity can be somewhat predicted if you know the temperature.

Notice that for humidity and temperature much like most cases of traditional regression, the "x" and "y" values are CONTINUOUS. Meaning they can take on any value. For example temperature can be

40 deg F

71.7 deg F

-31.66 deg F

Or any value in between.

We'll revisit this issue of continuous data again in a few paragraphs.

In this particular instance of regression analysis we want to see if a worker's gender, prior years of manufacturing experience and commute distance had any impact on the probability of them quitting in the time period since they were hired.

Below is a snap shot of part of the data table gathered:

commute distance	Gender (male=1)	prior yrs mfg experience	Did they leave (Left =1)
12	1	9	0
10	1	16	0
11	1	11	0
9	1	12	0
14	1	9	1
11	0	1	0
14	0	9	1
4	1	9	0
13	1	10	1
14	1	9	1
9	0	15	0
12	0	11	0
9	1	10	0
13	0	11	1

The hypothesis was:

Do any of the variables correlate with the fact that someone left the company or not?

I.e.—is there a correlation between: commute distance (in miles), gender, and prior yrs. mfg. experience in years (the "X"' independent variables) and if someone quit or not (the "Y" dependent variable)

Using Minitab —a common statistical software used in Six Sigma companies- one can do a Binary Logistic Regression.

Unlike traditional regression described above; logistic regression is when our "y" or dependent variable is DISCRETE.

Discrete data as contrasted to CONTINUOUS data mentioned above (I told you we would revisit this).

That means it can only take on a few values such as "quit the company =1" and "did not quit=0".

Discrete data comes in the form of

-Yes or No

-Pass or fail

-blue or green

-north, south, east or west

And like this case

-1 or 0 (1 being "quit" and 0 being "did not quit")

When we do the analysis we can see that "gender" and "work experience" are not statistically significant but that "commute distance" is-and we can get an equation that relates our "x" dependent variable of "commute distance" to our "y" or independent variable of "did they quit or not"

From a logistic regression equation, we can predict "what is the probability of someone quitting based on how long (in miles)was their commute distance.

Making a table in Excel, with commute distances going up to 30 miles (anything beyond that is unrealistic given the traffic in area around the plant):

commute distance	Probability of quitting
1	0.00%
2	0.00%
3	0.10%
4	0.10%
5	0.30%
6	0.40%
7	0.40%
8	0.60%
9	0.90%
10	1.00%
11	1.50%
12	18.24%
13	92.41%
14	99.86%
15	100.00%
16	100.00%

We can see from this that commute distance has little impact on the probability of someone quitting until the 12 mile mark where it is 18.24%.

And at the 13 mile mark (corresponds to a 30-45 min drive) it jumps to 92.41%

And beyond 13 miles it is almost assured that someone will quit.

What this seems to imply is that during the high hiring period the HR people and the hiring managers were very liberal about who they interviewed and hired for the new jobs.

Likewise applicants who applied probably didn't realize that the commute could be arduous and probably not cost effective given the price of gas and all.

Going forward, how long someone had to drive to get to the plant would be a factor that they should address in the interview process.

Now legal and general HR practices usually do not allow for direct hiring decisions based solely on where someone lives necessarily. But it is an issue that can be brought up with an applicant when delving into how reliable they might be to get to work on time and with good attendance.

And as any good HR professional will tell you (and as we shall see later in this book) attendance is perhaps the number one items in determining whether an employee (especially hourly employees) is considered a good and successful worker or not.

Someone living 25 miles away would logically be at a disadvantage than someone living only 5 miles away all other things being equal.

Tracking and analyzing attrition rates as you will see in a lot of these cases, is a big part of HR.

As is resolving conflicts between associates and supervisors. Below is just such a case

CASE STUDY 2: "Sometimes it really is the boss"

> MAN VS. MAN
>
> "Take this job and shove it"
>
> Johnny Paycheck
>
> (actually a song written
>
> by David Allan Coe)

An order entry group of 25 people process business to business orders from customers throughout the US, and then schedule product delivery from various plants to various customer sites. From January to September 2011, this group had an attrition rate of 42%.

This was not your generic order entry or call center type of operation. Unlike call centers that the general public is familiar with such as Amazon.com, or VISA credit card or when your cable goes out-this was an order entry environment which handles almost exclusively business-to-business sales of a commodity; the work is quite different.

It can be more technical, require different skill sets and is more of an inside sales type of position. As a result hiring and filling the individual contributor roles as well as the supervisory roles is much more challenging than your run of the mill customer call center.

In this case the team was divided into different regions of the country (Northeast, Midwest, etc.) and the people worked for 2 supervisors who in turn worked directly with each member day by day and hour by hour to track:

-number of orders entered.

-the number of calls abandoned and answered.

-time on the phone.

-time away from their desk.

Etc.

The team has 25 people working 8am-5PM EST Mon-Fri (a few weekends) at all times.

Or at least they attempt this schedule since due to training, vacations, attrition, etc. these number can vary.

36 people have worked there the year in question with 11 having quit within the same year.

Of the two supervisors; call them Betty and Veronica (fictitious names of course so not to be confused with the Archie's characters who by the way were great actresses)

- Betty covers regions that requires 15 representatives and she has had 3 that quit.

- Veronica covers regions that require 10 representatives and she has had 8 that quit.

So for all the 36 people who had cycled through:

- 20 went to Betty (of which 3 quit).

And

- 16 went to Veronica (of which 8 quit).

A common Six Sigma tool is a hypothesis test called a 2 proportion tests that compares the ratio of two proportions to determine if there is a statistically significant difference in the ratios. This is a perfect scenario for the application of this tool.

We have then

Betty: 3 out of a total of 20 leaving with in a year's time.

Veronica: 8 out of a total of 16 leaving within the same time frame.

Using Minitab software again gives us

Test and CI for Two Proportions

```
Supervisor      Number to quit      Total people       Sample p
Betty                 3                  20             0.150000
Veronica              8                  16             0.500000


Difference = p (1) - p (2)
Estimate for difference:  -0.35
95% CI for difference:    (-0.640710, -0.0592904)
Test for difference = 0 (vs not = 0):   Z = -2.36   P-Value = 0.018
```

Comparing Betty's attrition (3 out of 20 leaving) to Veronica's (8 out of 16) leaving and this shows that the odds of this happening by chance along is only 1.8%.

Or very unlikely. Something else is clearly at play here than just normal variation of attrition rate between the two supervisors.

This implies that Veronica has some issue with attrition that is unique and different from Betty.

Exit interviews, HR one-on-one interviews began to reveal this root cause of the problem.

Apart from normal personality conflicts and micro-managing, Veronica was not technical competent enough on the database system (Oracle) that all the representatives were working on and as a result she could not pull her weight (although this was a supervisory position it did require doing some of the order entry work and providing technical guidance to others) and this was causing a major rift among her team.

Fortunately this was salvageable and with 3-4 weeks of training Veronica was brought up to speed technically and in the following 6 months in 2012 only experienced 1 person leaving, thereby bringing the attrition rate back down to historic normal levels.

No further attention from Human Resources was needed at this point.

None of this could have been discovered without using the Measure/Analyze Phase of the Six Sigma DMAIC (Define, Measure, Analyze, Improve, and Control) problem solving methodology.

It had previously been viewed as just bad hires, personality conflicts, high stress working conditions, and a micro-managing boss.

Once definitive metrics were put in place and some statistical inference applied, the real root cause was unearthed.

As mentioned in the very beginning of this book, sometimes a manufacturing plant has a problem and they don't even realize that it is an HR problem at its core.

The next case is a case of a HR problem presenting as a quality problem, and sending a lot of engineers and technicians scrambling and trouble- shooting when in the end it should have been the VP of HR who could have solved it from the inception.

CASE STUDY 3: "Why would I work nights for nuttin?"

MAN VS. HIS NATURE

"Work your fingers to the bone

and what do you get-boney

fingers"

Hoyt Axton

A Tier 1 auto supplier to Ford, GM and Chrysler produced probes and valves that detect carbon dioxide (CO_2) in an automobile's exhaust system and provide feedback to a car's internal computer on how well the engine is performing.

This facility of about 300 people is located in a very small town in middle of OH. Surrounded by lots of farms and Amish country, it is one of few industrial facilities within a thirty minute drive.

This was a non-union shop that made high volume parts with a consistent schedule. Usually overtime on Sat. was necessary to meet production even though the main customers (the auto manufacturers) discourage having a process that requires regular overtime.

During a 6 month period of time in 2012, it was determined via customer returns, increase in warranty claims and end of line (EOL) audits that the scrap rate had sky rocketed to over 17%. This was up from a historic norm of 5-8%.

With a scrap rate like that, they were in danger of losing their status as a preferred auto supplier and with that loss would bring arduous inspections and a lot of manual costly audits of each part.

That could cripple this $600M operation. They had to get their quality issues under control immediately.

Since the parts were serialized, they could determine from the rejected parts, what date/time they were produced. Oddly over 90% of the scrapped items were made after 2:30PM every day.

All the parts were made by a cell of fourteen different stations. Three of the stations were considered to require a lot of operator expertise in terms of machine interaction and quick judgment calls on the sequence of robotic steps.

The plant operated on three shifts that ran as:

- Days 6AM-2PM.
- Swing 2PM-10PM.
- Mids 10PM-6AM.

All things being equal one would expect from a statistical point of view that the rejected parts would be equally scattered throughout all the shifts.(i.e.-a third from each shift roughly).

Or at least distributed via the volume made during each shift (i.e.— if 1st shift made twice as many parts as 2nd shift , on average it could make twice as many defective parts). However this wasn't the case at all.

Day shift had very few rejected parts even though it made the most. Mid shift was by far the worse and it made the least amount of parts

Clearly "shift" was an important variable in the production of bad parts.

Upon further deep dive it could be determined that the 3 hardest stations were the source of an inordinate percentage of bad parts on both Swings and Mid shift.

As it so happened, the experience level on the back shifts was much lower than the experience level on Day shift.

In fact the reject rate seemed to track inversely with the experience level of the operator who happened to be working on the machine in question. In some cases a brand new person was put on the most complicated machine as their first job at the company sometimes within a few days of being hired. Clearly this was a recipe for disaster.

How was this allowed to happen?

One answer was clear: There was no "shift differential" pay scale at the plant. Meaning Swing and Mid shift paid the same rate as Day shift.

In general workers would prefer to work Days (with a few exceptions) than Swings or Mids.

As a result the more experienced, seasoned workers with more influence would eventually work their way to Day shift leaving less experienced and competent workers on the back shift.

With this shift in talent there was also a lowering of morale as quality dipped and pressure from management increased.

As a result more and more people on the back shifts quit thereby further reducing the experience to an unsustainable level as far as quality was concerned.

This, logically, caused Swing and Mid shift to have lower quality output than did Days.

Further inflaming this scenario was the absolute pay scale.

I found out this was a problem inadvertently by talking to a receptionist at the local hotel where I stayed while in town. She had recently left the plant for the hotel receptionist job because she made more money. She also directed me to a former coworker who worked at a fast food restaurant nearby who also left for more money.

A hotel receptionist and a fast food position both paid more money than a Tier 1 auto supplier to the major car companies?

Turns out that this Tier 1 auto supplier was only paying its workers approximately $8/hr. which was in line or lower than service and fast food jobs nearby.

In comparison workers on a Detroit assembly line or Toyota plant can make up to $20-$25/hr. in some cases.

Why would someone work night shift in a factory where the work was more difficult when they would command the same wage working days at other enterprises?

Since this particular company was under a lot of financial strain from customers and a parent company, just raising wages did not seem to be a very appealing recommendation for me, as consultant, to put forth.

However I was able to show that with a 20% increase in general wages, and adding a shift differential for 2nd and 3rd shifts, they should be able to reduce their reject rate to such a level (the current 17% down to the lower 5% where it used to be) that it was a net positive for the company.

In the end this was exactly the course the leadership took and projected into 2013 they appear to be on track to achieve a 2-3% ROI (Return on Investment)for this HR change.

Without a Six Sigma approach that first discovered the rising part reject rate (via a Statistical Process Control-SPC-chart) and then a further deep dive into the issue, the fact that this was an HR problem at the core might never have ever been discerned.

The company had spent a lot of time examining the technical operation of the robot program, the machines, the materials coming from the supplier, and a variety of other possible reasons for the reject rate.

Only by breaking the reject data into time and hence shifts, and then knowing that shift differences almost always imply personnel; could we then see that the root cause was a Human Resource problem.

CASE STUDY 4: VETTING IS GOOD

MAN VS. HIS PAST

> "I would never join a club that would have me as a member"
>
> Groucho Marx.

In Northwest Arkansas there isn't much to do or many places to work other than Walmart headquarters.

A large rural area that only has an airport due to Walmart's nearby corporate headquarters in Bentonville; it is home to a lot of farms, largely migrant workforce that doesn't seem to stay in one place for too long.

A factory there that produces media for filters hires approximately 300-400 people for a 3 shift operation. With 3 large furnaces, inside the factory the temperature in the summer time could easily reach 120 deg F for days.

In 2010 the company closed a factory in Oklahoma and another in Texas and several key people, both factory and salaried, were relocated to Arkansas to join this particular plant. Likewise a lot of production volume came to this plant thereby requiring a need to hire many more factory/hourly workers.

The new HR manager started in March but the need for hourly workers was more immediate so there was a ramp up of workers starting in late 2009 and Jan 2010.

That's when the problems started.

A plant like this where the conditions were hot, dirty, monotonous and where the local workforce was transient, turnover was always high. In fact 20-25% was not uncommon.

But recently in some months it had reached 40-50%.

Most of the turnover was in the form of workers just not coming back.

REASON FOR LEAVING	% OF TOTAL
voluntarily quit	42.00%
Attendance issues	20.00%
performance related	12.00%
laid off	10.00%
retired	8.00%
medical leave	6.00%
not authorized to work in US	2.00%

What this does is leaves the company in a very bad situation. It can take weeks to train workers on certain operations, and when they leave suddenly and there is a 24/7 need for product, that creates the problem of meeting customer demand. As a result, the factory was feeling a lot of pressure from their corporate office in New York.

They had always had people quit even suddenly but not at this rate.

What may have happened?

One thought was that it was gender related. In a lot of factories in the U.S., traditionally jobs requiring a lot of manual labor in arduous conditions were most often times filled by men.

However nowadays this isn't done and this view is considered (rightfully so) as quaint at best and illegally sexist at worse.

So the company now took measures to insure gender wasn't used in hiring.

Could it be that women were more likely to quit working in a hot, dirty factory in the summer time?

What the data showed:

60 TOTAL HIRED	18 PEOPLE ARE GONE	42 PEOPLE STAYED
11 FEMALE	5 FEMALE	6 FEMALE
49 MALE	13 MALE	36 MALE

Students of Six Sigma may recognize this as the format for a hypothesis test known as a Chi-Square.

A discrete data hypothesis test with 2 or more variables.

A Minitab analysis reveals:

Chi-Square Test: left, stayed

Expected counts are printed below observed counts
Chi-Square contributions are printed below expected counts

```
        left    stayed   Total
   1      5        6       11
         3.30    7.70
         0.876   0.375

   2     13       36       49
        14.70    34.30
         0.197    0.084

Total   18       42       60

Chi-Sq = 1.532, DF = 1, P-Value = 0.216
```

Since the p-value is > .05 (p=.216) this shows that there is NO statistically significant relationship between gender and attrition.

Meaning that, no, women were not more likely to quit than men despite the bad working conditions (another stereotype killed by the data)

A similar analysis with "Ethnic code" showed the same result. Gender and ethnicity were not behind the high turnover rate. The problem lied elsewhere.

Digging deeper, we looked at when the employees were hired over the previous year.

Date of Hire	Number of people hired that DOH
1/22/2012	7
4/29/2012	1
5/27/2012	1
6/10/2012	2
6/19/2012	1
6/24/2012	9
7/1/2012	4
7/8/2012	1
7/15/2012	4
7/22/2012	5
7/29/2012	4
9/18/2012	1
10/7/2012	2
10/21/2012	3
11/2/2012	1
11/11/2012	1
11/16/2012	2
11/27/2012	1

Then we examined out of these people who were hired, how many have quit within 90 days since 90 days is when an employee went off probation. Most workers hire in from a temp agency and after 90 days they can go from temp worker to full-time employee.

DATE OF HIRE	TOTAL	LEFT	STAYED	attrition
11/16/2012	12	1	11	8.33%
6/24/2012	9	5	4	55.56%
1/22/2012	7	3	4	42.86%
7/22/2012	5	4	5	80.00%
7/1/2012	4	2	2	50.00%
7/15/2012	4	2	2	50.00%
7/29/2012	4	0	4	0.00%
10/21/2012	3	0	3	0.00%
6/10/2012	2	0	2	0.00%
10/7/2012	2	0	2	0.00%
4/29/2012	1	1	0	100.00%
5/27/2012	1	0	1	0.00%
6/19/2012	1	0	1	0.00%
7/8/2012	1	0	1	0.00%
9/18/2012	1	0	1	0.00%
11/2/2012	1	0	1	0.00%
11/11/2012	1	0	1	0.00%
11/27/2012	1	0	1	0.00%

Notice that certain days that people were hired seem to have an abnormal attrition rate.

To make this more clear let's put the data into months rather than individual days

MONTH OF HIRE	
JAN	42.86%
FEB	
MAR	
APR	100.00%
MAY	0.00%
JUN	41.67%
JUL	44.44%
AUG	
SEP	0.00%
OCT	0.00%
NOV	6.67%

Clearly some months produced a large hiring of employees who could not make it past 90 days.

(Note: April only had one person hired and they quit and that is why April is listed at 100%. But this is hardly a sign of a problem for April).

Not coincidently the new HR manager did not start till March and a second HR person was hired in Sept.

This implies that the people doing the interviews during the months with the high attrition rate were not that adept at "vetting" or interviewing and picking out people who were more likely to stay on and be good, productive reliable workers.

In fact the more people you hire at any one time, the more likely it is that you will bring in a worker who won't last.

And if you have people who are not that experienced at HR interviewing and vetting techniques, this increases even more.

So at what point in this case do we limit how many people we interview and bring in? What is our "interviewing capacity" in other words?

Taking this same data we can put it into the following format:

TOTAL Hired	LEFT under 90 days	attrition. Yes =1
12	1	1
9	5	1
7	3	1
5	4	1
4	2	1
4	2	1
4	0	0
3	0	0
2	0	0
2	0	0
1	1	1
1	0	0
1	0	0
1	0	0
1	0	0
1	0	0
1	0	0
1	0	0

The more advanced Six Sigma Black Belt students might recognize this format as a Binary Logistic Regression. Just as we covered in an early Case Study a few chapters back.

Minitab produces the following output for this analysis:

Response Information

Variable	Value	Count	
attrition. Yes =1	1	7	(Event)
	0	11	
	Total	18	

Logistic Regression Table

Predictor	Coef	SE Coef	Z	P	Odds Ratio	95% CI Lower	Upper
Constant	-3.64877	1.59997	-2.28	0.023			
TOTAL Hired	1.05177	0.496097	2.12	0.034	2.86	1.08	7.57

Log-Likelihood = -6.160
Test that all slopes are zero: G = 11.737, DF = 1, P-Value = 0.001

From this we can get the equation (see past example of Binary Logistic Regression):

Probability of leaving = p

(p/p+1) = e^{ -3.64877 + (1.05177 *total people hired) }

We can take this and reduce it to a more easily deciphered analysis regarding the probability of someone quitting

total hired at one time	p% that will leave
1	6.92%
2	17.51%
3	37.76%
4	63.41%
5	83.20%
6	93.40%
7	97.59%
8	99.14%
9	99.70%
10	99.89%
11	99.96%
12	99.99%
13	100.00%
14	100.00%
15	100.00%

Notice that there is a very large jump in the probability of someone leaving when the number of people being hired goes from 3 to 4.

If we bring in 3 people there is only a 37.76% one of them will leave before 90 days.

Whereas if we bring in 4 people all of a sudden that probability of just one of them leaving in 90 days jumps dramatically to over 50% all the way to **63.41%**.

What this tells us is that HR personal need to be:

-well trained in how to interview to spot a potential worker's attendance, consistency, and staying with a job.

-trained and in sufficient number in order to handle a large influx of interviewees when a hiring up tick is needed.

-limit the number of people being interviewed and hired at any one time in order to lower the odds of increased attrition from the same said people.

Just opening the door and bringing in anyone off the streets just because you have a head count you need to fill is a very poor strategy and counter-productive as this Case shows.

CASE 6: The Making of Chewing Gum:

MAN VS. MACHINE

> "Tied to a wheel, fingers got to feel.."
>
> "Machinehead" by Bush

Bubble gum and chewing gum, believe it or not, is big business.

Billions of dollars each year spent by consumers on a variety of flavors and types. Maybe it wouldn't be if people could see how it is made (that is probably true for any food and drink I suspect).

As you might imagine to meet that demand, gum has to be mass produced via some type of machinery.

When you pass a lot of a sticky substance like gum through metallic parts in a very fast paced manner, it can really "gum up" the works (sorry, I couldn't resist the pun.)

In the Midwest a large manufacturing company with over 1500 employees working a 24/7 manner was finding this out the hard way.

A non-union shop under threat of union implementation was having problems meeting customer demand.

They had 4 teams that rotated working 12 hr. shifts on 14 different machines.

There was a lot of employee morale problems due to the 12 hr. shifts where some people could never get off weekends or worked 3 out of 4 weekends.

At the time the throughput efficiency was only 65% meaning that of 100 potential pieces of gum that started into the packaging process only 65 ready packaged pieces came out. It was calculated that if they could get the efficiency up to 70% they could go to just an 8 hr., two shift system giving more time off for the workers and saving money for the company

Here's how this worked:

- the gum which yes, is like literal rubber, is "cooked" in the form of rectangle slab that will later be cut into small pieces that you are familiar with when you buy gum in the store.

- The rectangle slabs are then taken to one of the fourteen machines that make two cuts, once along one line, then perpendicularly across another. The cut pieces then move along an assembly line, and then are quickly wrapped in a piece of paper. Several paper pieces are packaged into the overall final package you are used to seeing in a retail store.

- the final packages are then boxed up and sent to the dock ready for shipping.

The point where the gum is cut the last time and wrapped in paper is the problem area.

Over 2,000 pieces of gum can be moved and wrapped in 1 minute in these machines. This is faster than the human eye can see. A camera must be used and the frames slowed down in order to see what is actually going on.

In this case what was happening is that the gum has to enter into the machine in correct alignment in order to move through the rotating metallic parts where it then meets and is wrapped by the paper.

Over time the gum due to its high speed of motion gets out of align and due to its sticky nature, can become impinged on the metallic parts and this stops or slows down the whole process.

At this point, an operator must stop the machinery, open up the gear box and clear out the jam by either removing paper, cleaning off residual gum or a variety of other trouble shooting methods.

This happens about every 5-20 minutes over the course of an hour each and every hour of the day.

It should be clear that the operators that are experienced and very adept at finding and correcting the problem of the jammed machinery can bring the process back up more quickly and this will improve the overall efficiency and throughput of the line.

The 14 machines were all of German origin and when the German engineers installed them over 5 years ago they left them in a condition where they are able to achieve 90% efficiency.

Even as recently as 6 months prior, three engineers from the founding company came and was able to get to 83% efficiency on the two lines they worked on for nearly a month.

The factory then was under achieving and it was costing them money and putting a hardship on their employees.

The engineers in the U.S. at the plant knew that the efficiency varied with gum type, as some gum is a lot stickier than other brands. The more sticky the gum, the more clogs in the gears of the machinery you can expect.

They also knew that certain machines were a lot better than other machines of the 14 total that they had.

Also well-known was that some operators were better than others.

But which of these variables were most important and by how much? Knowing this could lead them to make the necessary changes perhaps to get them to the 70% needed efficiency.

Each 1% point movement on efficiency saved approximately $250K according to their finance department.

Data was captured by PLC's (Program Logic Controllers) on each of the machines. The machines can know how many pieces of gum it wrapped and at what time.

This gives us the: machine, the operator (each operator wands in via a bar code reader on their badge as soon as they start work), pieces produced, time, reason (out of a few given choices) it was down, where the fault was, and a variety of other parameters.

The data showed on thing that was obvious right away:

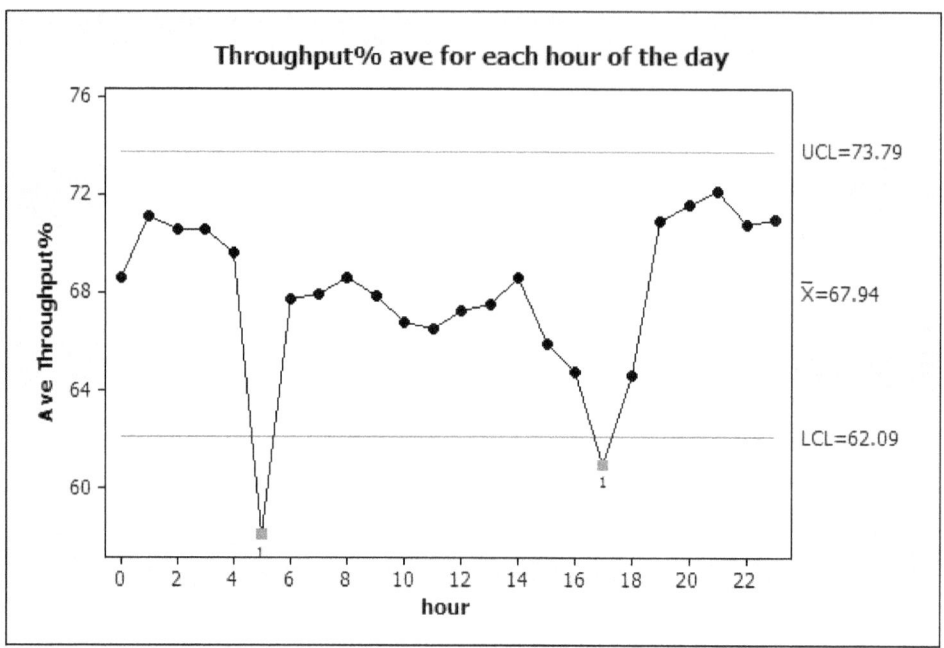

This is based on data taken over the past 6 months. It shows the Average throughput% each hour over that time

Notice the dramatic drops in efficiency at

- 0500 or 5:00AM
- 1700 or 5:00PM

As was mentioned the work force works in 12 hr. shifts on four different teams.

Turns out that they turnover at 5am and 5pm each day.

So one team comes in at 5am and works 12 hours then another team comes in and takes over. The turn over to the team occurs at 5pm. 12 hours later the cycle repeats with a shift change and turnover at 5am.

And so on and so on.

This data shows an overall average throughput of 67.94%

But during the hours of 5am and 5pm that dropped down to 56% at 5am and 61% at 5pm

This is a very large drop in efficiency as you may imagine.

What was happening is that if a person was late relieving the current operator, the operator would just turn off the machinery and just leave so production went to zero before the next person came on and started it back up from scratch.

And who can blame them really since they would have been there for 12 hours and no doubt were tired and frustrated at not being able to leave on time.

OR

More often there was little or no communication between the off going operator and the oncoming operator on how the machines were working, any problems that may have occurred during the past 12 hrs.

This was one area they needed to clean up right away and should be an easy fix. (It wasn't and rarely is however).

By improving the turnover between shifts by both enforcing on time attendance, policies, what to go over, overall communication in general, the plant was able to get a quick win and make some improvements right away.

Within a few weeks the dips seen above went away and this alone saved $75K.

But that was the easy part.

The shift turnover loss was a small part of what was being left on the table in the loss in efficiency for the remaining 22 hours of the day.

The shift change over issue only brought the two particular hours in line with the rest of production and up the 67% throughput average. Still a long way to go.

They would have to solve the original problem of which variable was the biggest driver of product loss among:

   A. Machine
   B. Gum type
   C. Operator

Machine difference was clear from this data over a 6 month period:

Machine	Ave Throughput%	Category
GGW01	80.17	B1
RGW01	79.47	B2
AGW01	75.10	B3
QGW01	73.87	B4
EGW01	64.92	
CGW01	63.77	
BGW01	62.87	
DGW01	62.41	
PGW01	61.09	
FGW01	59.26	W4
OGW01	58.11	W3
SGW01	57.86	W2
HGW01	56.41	W1

(Note: one machine was down during this period so only 13 were running when the data was captured).

(Note 2: I have used the terms "BOB" for "Best of the Best" and "WOW" for "Worse of the Worse").

This shows the best machines such as B1, B2, etc. As well as the worse machines labeled as "W1, W2, etc.

It is a common problem solving method to identify the best and worst performers on any given activity and then break down the common characteristics of each and the characteristics that are the greatest difference between the BOB's and WOW's are most likely the same ones that are driving the good and bad performers.

One machine was as good as 80.17% while another was as poor as 56.41%

This particular plant had about fifty different flavors of gum. Most made up a very small percentage of the volume. To make this analysis more meaningful overall we looked at only the brands that made up 80% of the volume. As per the Pareto principle (the 80/20 rule where 20% of some makes up 80% of the output of any process) about 20% of the gum flavors accounted for nearly 80% of the total volume of all the gum

In the data below I have changed the name of the flavors of the gum in order to avoid being to identify the brand and company. Instead of actual flavor of gum you would know from a store I just labeled them as "a", "b", etc. all lower case letters of the alphabet.

FLAVOR	Average of Throughput	Classification
c	87.58%	B1
b	86.57%	B2
a	76.75%	B3
d	76.37%	B4
e	73.69%	B5
h	65.82%	W5
g	59.88%	W4
i	58.54%	W3
f	54.63%	W2
j	50.98%	W1

One flavor, "c", ran very well in the machines to the point of an 87.58% throughput.

On the other end a flavor, "j", ran at 50.98%.

This is an enormous difference. After seeing this no one doubted that gum flavor was a big factor in determining the efficiency of the plant operations.

Who the operator was on the machine also was shown to be important as seen in the data below:

Operator	Average throughput	Classification
A	82.48%	B1
B	81.56%	B2
C	78.78%	B3
D	77.49%	B4
P	64.42%	W4
Q	62.94%	W3
R	61.27%	W2
S	56.56%	W1

Obviously I had to change the name of the operators in question. Instead I have them labeled as "A", "B", and capital letters of the alphabet.

The best operator performed at an 82.48% (BOB, B1) while the worse was at 56.56% (WOW, W1)

All three variables show a very wide diversity in performance. The real question is, are the machine efficiency numbers driven by who the operator is and or what gum flavor is being run?

Or is an operator's numbers being driven by the machine he is working on and the flavor of gum?

It would be grossly unfair to hold a particular operator responsible for having bad efficiency numbers if that operator too often ran bad gum on a bad machine.

Likewise why reward another operator for good performance when he/she happened to be working on a good running machine running a well running gum flavor.

How best to separate out the influence of each?

Especially given the data below that shows that an operator's performance was directly related to the number of lines they worked on.

What you see below is data in (once again) Binary Logistic Regression format. It shows the probability of a given operator making the goal of 70% throughput, during the past 6 months of work based on the number of lines that they worked on:

Number of lines worked	Probability of meeting goal
1	79.99%
2	66.62%
3	48.50%
4	30.77%
5	17.34%
6	9.01%
7	4.46%
8	2.16%
9	1.03%

Notice that the probability of an operator meeting the production goal of 70% throughput dipped below 50% if they worked on 3 or more lines.

What this was implying was that the more lines or machines an operator worked on, the less experienced they were at clearing the faults and jams of the machines. In other words being a "jack of all trades master of none" was a BAD thing in this scenario.

Apparently what may be needed was for operators to master 1-2 machines only rather than working on several.

But let's look at all the variables all at once before we jump to that conclusion.

Let's look at which of the variables between:

- Machine
- Flavor
- Operator

had the largest influence.

An astute Six Sigma Black Belt student may recognize this as a hypothesis test. Specifically since the data is continuous (throughput% can take on any value) and we have 2 or more variables (operator, machine and gum flavor) this is an ANOVA or Analysis of Variance.

This is where we not only see if there is a difference in the mean and variance between the variables but also the magnitude of the interactions.

In fact let's throw in the variable "Hour" since we saw earlier that the hour of the day was significant during shift change over, and then we can see which of the variables are the bigger drivers and their interactions.

We have then

    A- Line (or machine)
    B- Operator
    C- Flavor
    D- Hour

Putting this in Minitab and doing a General Linear Model ANOVA we have

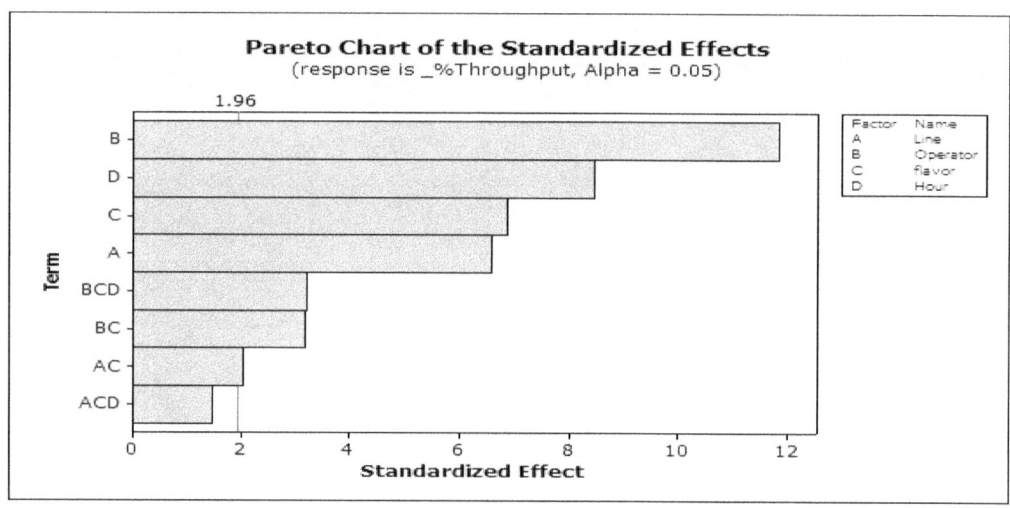

Which shows that all the variables are statistically significant including all the interactions EXCEPT:

AC → Line and flavor. Meaning that the machine the gum flavor ran on was not significant. That means that a particular gum flavor would run basically the same regardless of what machine it was run on.

ACD→ Line, flavor, hour. Just like above, the hour of the day ALSO didn't matter in how a particular gum flavor ran. A given gum flavor ran basically the same regardless of what machine or what hour of the day it ran.

To gauge the magnitudes (from the graph above we can see the bigger
impact variables but we can't quantify them from the picture alone) we
have the Minitab analysis:

* NOTE * There is partial confounding, no alias table was printed.

* NOTE * This design is not orthogonal.

Factorial Fit: _%Throughput versus Line, Operator, flavor, Hour

```
Estimated Effects and Coefficients for _%Throughput (coded units)

Term                    Effect     Coef   SE Coef       T       P
Constant                          60.927   1.0199   59.74   0.000
Line                     9.140    4.570    0.6951    6.57   0.000
Operator                15.303    7.652    0.6466   11.83   0.000
flavor                   7.045    3.523    0.5133    6.86   0.000
Hour                    16.803    8.402    0.9949    8.44   0.000
Line*flavor              6.192    3.096    1.5202    2.04   0.042
Operator*flavor         -9.617   -4.809    1.5010   -3.20   0.001
Line*flavor*Hour        -4.389   -2.195    1.4884   -1.47   0.140
Operator*flavor*Hour     9.641    4.820    1.4883    3.24   0.001


S = 21.7689     PRESS = 1092005
R-Sq = 25.38%   R-Sq(pred) = 24.61%    R-Sq(adj) = 25.11%
```


Operator and Hour are now the most impactful variables
2x as much as flavor and line

Significant variables ordered
By impact

FACTOR	DOE COEFFICIENT	abs coeff
Hour	8.4	8.4
Operator	7.65	7.65
oper*flavor*hr	4.82	4.82
oper*flavor	-4.8	4.8
Line	4.57	4.57
Flavor	3.52	3.52
line*flavor	3.1	3.1

Hour has the biggest impact and we know why from the earlier
discussion on shift change over.

But ***operator*** was the next largest driver.

Operator mattered more than ***flavor*** and ***line*** on how efficiency the plant ran.

In fact ***operator*** interaction with the ***flavor*** had a bigger impact than the ***line*** and or the ***flavor*** acting alone

-Line *Operator interaction is NOT significant so lines that perform well
  do so due to the operators not vice versa.

-Operator *flavor interaction has more impact than the Line*flavor
   Interaction.

-Operator* flavor interaction has more of an impact on what line is being
   run on and what flavor is being run at the time.

This tells us that to really make a big improvement on the throughput% we should be concentrating on operator.

Man matters more than machine or "matter" (gum flavor)in this case.

As in a lot of manufacturing problems this is the case. What is often times looked at as a machinery, technology or other issue is quite frequently an HR issue at the core.

But now that we know this, how do we fix it?

We have enough data to know that operator is the biggest driver.

We can also tell which machines which operators run the best on.

Currently as the plant operates, workers come in for their shift and just go to whichever machine they want to or that is open and then start their shift.

As we saw in a previous analysis, the number of lines an operator worked on, the less likely their throughput% would be up to the needed 70% standard.

But what if each operator went to the machine they performed the best on each shift? Wouldn't that be an immediate uptick in efficiency?

Below is the data for each operator on each machine and how they performed over the past 6 months

Row Labels	AGW01	BGW01	CGW01	DGW01	EGW01	FGW01	GGW01	HGW01	OGW01	PGW01	QGW01	RGW01	SGW01	Grand Total
A				28.60	73.51	43.79	66.49	74.66	64.14	64.66	62.03	75.39	79.40	67.90
B		66.81	86.97	90.85		77.96	53.63	82.06	63.61	67.20				72.38
C		58.29	75.11	70.83	66.06	80.88	56.93	71.73	54.18	60.99			58.65	65.35
D											80.27	67.80	70.07	72.91
E		82.17	93.49	67.22					67.45	54.89				69.48
F								51.81			63.32	68.10		64.42
G					46.16	64.86		41.81				62.67		56.56
H		60.88	86.73	78.00	64.97	65.38		70.95	64.85	70.48				70.85
I		72.75	78.91	43.64			67.78				74.00	83.59	78.57	74.68
J		69.16						95.48			77.57	79.71	81.90	81.56
K			57.03						62.23		63.12			62.94
L								60.77			69.19	79.52	80.50	78.78
M			98.52	65.30	52.59		61.24	65.17	54.86	80.94				61.27
N		65.79	87.22		80.77				55.68	68.63	71.06		71.76	70.32
O		46.94	91.48	83.57	72.01	73.58		80.56	76.42	76.67	56.81		72.31	74.51
P			61.59	69.86		79.52			49.44	80.38				68.90
Q											82.54	77.29		82.48
R		62.74	81.68	72.09	63.28	78.02	63.48	63.09	66.82	72.44				65.18
S			92.14	72.63	71.68	73.76	88.01			46.31				77.49
(blank)														
Grand Total		65.01	83.43	69.17	64.54	72.14	65.38	69.97	61.42	68.94	62.70	79.28	76.14	80.18	71.79

Just putting the operators on their best machines in and of itself alone would have raised the throughput% average to 71.79% above the goal of 70% which they needed to go to 8 hr. shifts and get off the 12 hr. shifts 24/7

If 1% saves $250K as per their finance, then this moves them from their average over the past year of 65% to 71.79% equals -→ $1.7M approximately

Just putting the right people in the right spots can give that much savings.

Of course making this happen in reality is easier said than done. Some people share the same machine as their best. Some people call in sick and a supervisor can't cover each machine if each person can only operator one machine, and etc. on a variety of other variables that make this a hard thing to schedule.

Using the data above and aligning people with their best machines first, then backups and if necessary a secondary back up we can produce a schedule that looks like:

	Primary person	Back-up	secondary backup
AGW01	E	I	
BGW01	M	E	S
CGW01	B	O	
DGW01	N	A	
EGW01	C	P	
FGW01	S	I	
GGW01	J	B	
HGW01	R	H	
OGW01	P	R	
PGW01	K	N	
QGW01	Q	D	
RGW01	I	J	
SGW01	L	A	J

This gives a supervisor some flexibility on how to deploy the operators that show up on each shift. This also allows planning for vacations, and other known periods when certain people have to be gone.

Note that during this whole analysis we didn't even dive into what made certain people good on certain machines and certain people bad on others. Nor why certain flavors of gum performs so bad (other than it is stickier).

We just used the resources that we had and used them in a more efficient manner.

We improved the shift change over.

We identified the best operators on the best machines and deployed them accordingly.

This alone was sufficient to drive the throughput average to the goal of > 70%.

The next step would have been to MOVE the throughput performance of EVERY operator by identifying key trouble shooting methods, making small adjustments to the machines themselves, and the gum texture itself, and other heuristic methods.

But just using our current HR resources we were able to reach the goal.

In a case of man vs machine, just using "man" helped us reach our goal.

In the next few chapters I will go over various scenarios rather than actual Case studies, to show some peculiar issues that may arise in a HR context, where Six Sigma Tools can help one analyze what is truly going on. Here we will separate data and fact, from perception and myth.

SCENARIO 1: Reward and punishment and a random walk

MAN VS. TIME

"Do not waste time, for it is the stuff life is made of"

Ben Franklin

It is a common view of many managers and supervisors, that rewarding good behavior and punishing bad behavior will get you're the desired behavior from an employee.

If an associate does something wrong like coming in late, punish them via docking their pay, suspension, public ridicule, stocks, tar and feather and up to even termination as necessary in some cases.

Likewise give out trinkets; McDonald's gifts cards or what have you should they come in on time or even early in a consistent manner.

Makes sense right?

Well let's consider this scenario:

Say an employee is supposed to be at work at 8am. One day he is late and comes in at 8:15am.

The supervisor being a fair guy figures maybe he had a flat tire so lets it slide.

Say the next day he comes in at 8:30am. Way too late for the supervisor to turn his head now, he must take action! So he gives the employee a verbal warning.

The following day the employee improves but is still late at 8:15am. The supervisor thinks that he is getting better and just hasn't fully turned it around from the verbal lambasting he just got yesterday so reminds him that the company is losing its patience.

Sure enough the following day the employee is on time at 8am.

Supervisor feels vindicated.

In fact the very next day the employee is even EARLY at 7:45am

After that he comes in at 7:30am. The supervisor is so impressed that he gives him an "atta-boy" and a gift certificate to midnight bowling at the desert bowling alley on the outskirts of town near the toxic waste dump.

A few days later employee comes in at 8am, but then he falls back into his old bad habits and comes in at 8:15am. Late again.

Since he was doing so well the supervisor again lets it slide but sure enough, the following day it's 8:30 when the supervisor sees the employee meandering in.

That's it! He thinks. This time he is given a written notice in his permanent file locked away in the HR permanent file safe deep in the bowels of the company store room

That will teach him!

And apparently it does. The employee is in at 8:15, followed by on time at 8am after that.

A few days later he's even early at 7:30am prompting the supervisor to give him another award this time a t-shirt with the company logo and inspirational theme motto on the front and back.

But alas it is for naught as the employee starts getting later and later till he's coming in at 8:30 again.

The whole process is repeated.

Now what is the supervisor to think?

He notices that every time he punishes the employee his behavior improves

Every time he rewards him his behavior gets worse.

The supervisor can't help but deduce that punishment is way more of a productive "good" tool than reward and praise. I.e. —it does more good to punish an employee and rewarding them just makes them lax. So let's keep the punishment and get rid of the rewards. Keep the stick, lose the carrot if you will.

What do you think a view like that will have on the supervisor and employee going forward?

But what is really going on here?

Consider this—

Isn't the graph below really what is going on with the employee's arrival time?

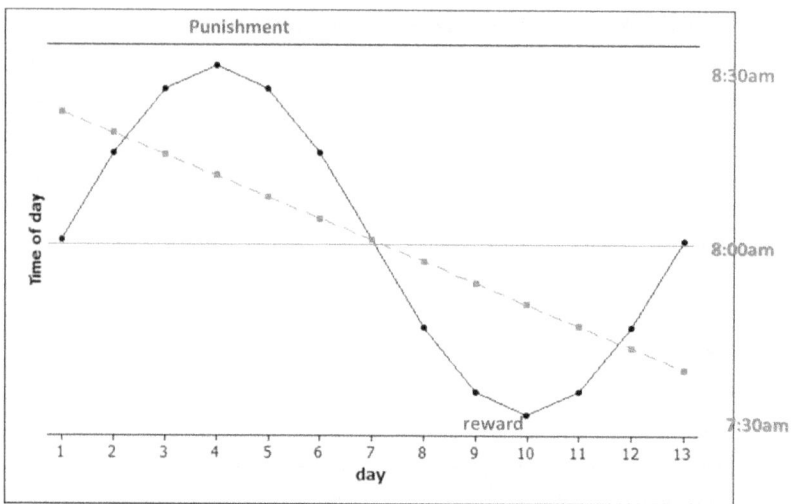

Those of you who can remember back in geometry class will recognize this pattern as just a standard sine wave.

In other words- the employees arrival time is based on a given frequency (in this case it happens to be a sine wave) and has NOTHING TO DO WITH PUNISHMENT OR REWARD. It is totally random.

Minitab even put in a regression line (red line) showing a downward trend. But there really is no trend at all as it is random.

The supervisor thinks he is altering the situation by moving the arrival time back toward the target of 8am when in reality, the arrival time is just moving what way it does soley due to the nature of the pattern.

Likewise, the supervisor is mistaken in his view that rewarding the employee just makes him behave worse therefore rewards are ineffective-this is also an error since after the reward the arrival time just follows the normal pattern back toward the target.

Notice also that the supervisor's punishments and rewards are well timed. In that the punishments occur right at the peak of the bad behavior and the rewards happen right at the apex of the best behavior. This acts to solidify the fallacy of the supervisor's incorrect interpretation of the events.

Now in this scenario the pattern may be an unlikely one found in real life. While electrical current, magnetism and other items in physics commonly follow a sine wave patter, few times do we see human activity so demonstrated.

But this fallacy is an example of a bigger phenomenon called "regression to the mean".

It is the phrase "regression to the mean" that the correlation analysis of "regression" in general gets its name.

What is "regression to the mean?"

From Wikipedia:

http://en.wikipedia.org/wiki/Regression_toward_the_mean

"Regression toward (or to) the mean is the phenomenon that if a variable is extreme on its first measurement, it will tend to be closer to the average on its second measurement—and, paradoxically, if it is extreme on its second measurement, it will tend to have been closer to the average on its first. To avoid making wrong inferences, regression toward the mean must be considered when designing scientific experiments and interpreting data".

In other words, Shaq, who is 7'1" will probably have a son who is SHORTER than he is, because he's son-while he maybe tall- will probably be a height that is more closer to the average height of men. Say 5'9".

That is, his son's height will "regress" or move closer to the average value from the extreme value of his dad's height.

In our scenario, whenever the employee arrived very late, say at 8:30am, it is probable that his next arrival time will be closer to the average (or target) of 8am.

Likewise when he is early at 7:30am, the next day he will probably get there closer to 8am.

We see this a lot in sports. A player will have a great year and the following year it won't be so good and right away fans will conclude that the player is losing his ability. Be it age, other competitors "figuring him out" (which could be true), the player not being as dedicated and "resting on his laurels" so to speak.

None of that could be true and it could just be regression to the mean

The phrase "sophomore jinx" comes from this effect where a freshman has a great year and his sophomore year he doesn't seem quite so good.

What are we to take away from this? I mean what was the supervisor supposed to do?

Well the supervisor and anyone in general, would be well served by rigorously TRACKING and recording the exact arrival times of the employee each day for successive days.

This does two things:

1. From an HR point of view it documents the behavior which is needed whenever management has a complaint against an employee should that be the case.

2. He can see the pattern forming and realize that a sine wave (or whatever) is developing and that he must change the SYSTEM and not just act at individual extreme points.

Maybe the employee's alarm clock has some odd defect in it?

Maybe he comes to work on a traffic path that has construction going on and it varies like this?

Etc.

Who knows?

The point is that once the pattern is seen the supervisor can make decisions based on changing the system in general

This just goes to show you that in HR like all other disciplines data capture and analysis is essential

SCENARIO 2: Lie Detector and Drug Tests-Are they reliable?

MAN VS. MORALITY

"History is a set of lies agreed upon"

Napoleon Bonaparte

If you work in HR, at some time or another you will have run across lie detector tests or drugs test one way or another.

It is common for companies nowadays to have pre-employment drug screens and in some cases a polygraph (lie detector).

If you expect to work for a federal government agency associated with national security or intelligence or a contractor of said groups, you definitely will have to undergo a polygraph.

Several states make it illegal for any private company to require a polygraph as a condition of employment, but those states are in the minority.

Most companies conduct pre-employment drug screens as a requirement for insurance or health care reasons. Especially if the position involves something involving public safety like truck/bus driver, handling money, or other public safety positions.

The theory of a polygraph is that It measures blood pressure, respiration, skin conductivity (as a function of sweating), and heart rate. (since it measures many things it has many graphs, hence the name "poly"-graph). It is thought that if a person is lying, they will feel guilty or something in such a way that it will alter their bodily functions along these 4 metrics one way or another. I.e., they will sweat, breath differently, pulse rate changes all different from a baseline measurement.

That is why a polygraph first establishes a baseline by asking the participant to answer some questions truthfully such as: your name, age, location, other information that can be verified.

THEN, ask them to deliberately lie. It does this via a pre-screen where the polygrapher asks the participant to think of a time when they may have lied, cheated, stolen or what have you, then have the person think of that time and deliberately lie.

In this way the polygrapher can capture the bodily response of the person when they tell the truth and when they knowingly lie.

A polygraph only asks "YES" or "NO" questions. The person being tested never answers anything other than a "YES" or "NO".

So when they ask a question on which they are probing, they can tell if the person is lying or not by how close their response is to either their baseline truth state or their baseline lying state

Or so they say.

I have had my own personal experience with a Counter-Intel polygraph while working with a defense contractor where we were involved in overhead spy satellite program.

A Counter-Intel poly in the Black Ops security world polygraph differs from a Life Style Polygraph.

In a Counter-Intel polygraph they only ask you questions regarding your involvement with foreign governments or people, whether you have perhaps told others about your work, or other criminal acts or treason.

A Life Style Poly is much more intrusive. Questions involved your sexual practices and views, personal intimate thoughts on loved ones and others, how you interact with pets and animals (yeah. Believe it or not), and other odd items.

People who are going to be deployed in the field, meaning spies or working as diplomats in foreign countries are giving the Life Style Poly.

I didn't lie in my Counter Intel poly but it took 2 sessions at 4 hours each before they agreed that yep "No Signs of Deception" were present. This after a QA (Quality Audit) team looked at the results for days. (This is a normal result for most people by the way.)

At beginning the polygrapher asked me to pick a number between 1-5. I picked 3. He then wrote out the numbers 1-5 and wrote the number 3 extra-large. He put this paper with the written numbers in front of me and said "when I ask you if you picked number 3, I want you to say 'No'".

He also asked me to think about a time in my life when I actually did lie, and that I felt bad about doing it.

He then asked me to think about that time as he asked me about that specific instance. He told me to deliberately lie. This was to establish what my body reactions were to a known lie.

Using that information we went back to the number I picked between 1-5.

We went through this exercise and then he showed me a graph and said "See, this showed that you lied when you said you didn't pick 3" because the graphs were similar to when we know you lied (as he had requested) about the thing from your past.

THAT is what he passed off as "proof" of the accuracy of the polygraph.

A better test would be to have me, **secretly**, pick a number between 1-100 and write it down and do NOT show it to him.

Then by using a convergence method of asking 7 questions, he would get to the right answer IF he could tell if I were really lying.

What I mean is, he would ask

1. Is your number between 51-100? I answer YES or NO and if he can tell if I lied he can ask the next question
2. Is your number between 25-50?
3. Is your number between 13-24
4. Is your number between 7-12
5. Is your number between 4-6?
6. Is your number between 2-3
7. Is your number 1-2

For instance, let's say the number is 61.

Question 1: Is your number between 51-100?-→ Answer: YES

Since it's a polygraph he can tell my "YES" answer is correct

Question 2: Is your number between 51-75? (half way to 100. I cut the total numbers available in half with each question. This is called Convergent Problem Solving). -→ Answer: YES

Question 3: Is your number between 51-63? (Again half way between 51 and 75 since I know the number lies there). -→ Answer: YES

Question 4: Is your number between 51-57? Answer-→ NO

So I now know the number is between 58 (from last question) and 63 (question 3)

Question 5: Is your number between 58-61? (This is roughly half the remaining numbers). Answer-→YES

Question 6: Is your number between 58-60? Answer-→NO

Question 7: Is your number 61? Answer-→ Yes

Which we already know to be true if all the above answers are truthful OR in the case where they are not, a poly-grapher can tell that they are not truthful.

And if the person administering the test can tell a truth from a lie, then they will know the true answer to each of the question above.

By following this method and knowing if the person is lying or not, a polygrapher can ascertain what my secret number is without having me write it out in front of him before-hand.

If the polygraph test were 90% accurate and if it requires 7 questions to get to a number picked between 1-100, then he has a 48% chance of getting it right.

This is derived by:

$(.90)^7 = .48$

Or

Question 1 accuracy - 90%

Question 2 accuracy - 90%

Question 3 accuracy - 90%

and so on for

$(.90) * (.90) * (.90) …. (.90)$ —for a total of seven times.

If we did this test say 6 independent times then at least 2-3 times (48% of 6) we can expect him to exactly determine my number.

When I suggested this he of course dismissed it as being too lengthy and taking too long. Which, although maybe true, it turned out we would be in there for 4 hours on a lot less than 7 question anyway and under dubious justification for accuracy.

But be that as it may.

Most polygraphers who work for the US government are trained at the National Center for Credibility Assessment at Ft. McClellan, Alabama run by the U. S. Army.

There they are taught that the polygraph in the hands of an experienced and well trained person can be between 85--90% accurate.

So they say.

And drug tests are even more accurate. In fact few people doubt the accuracy of drug tests.

Which brings us back around to the issue.

Question:

"If a polygraph (or drug test) is 90% accurate and given to 10,000 people of which 10% are lying , guilty or taking drugs, what then is the odds that the person is indeed lying, guilty or taking drugs?"

At first glance this seems like an easy answer. (You may have seen this type of example in other books or articles.) Most people would readily say "well of course 90%" or something like that.

But if you have knowledge of Bayesian probability theory, you know the answer is a lot more complicated.

Let's look at the math behind this scenario:

-10,000 are tested.

- 90% is the accuracy of the test. This means that if you are guilty, then 90% of the time the test will show you as guilty. Likewise if you are innocent, then 90% of the time it will know that as well.

-Likewise, if you are guilty 10% of the time you will get away with it. And 10% of the time if you are innocent it will incorrectly call you guilty. Or a false positive.

The original crux of the question is "…what are the odds that the person is indeed guilty if the test says they are?"

Well if 10,000 take the test and 10% are truly guilt, then this breaks down as

- 9,000 innocent people
- 1,000 guilty people

Of the 9,000 innocent people, 90% or **8,100 will be called innocent and 900 innocent people will be incorrectly called GUILTY (false positives).**

The 1,000 guilty people will break down as—900 correctly called guilty and 100 guilty people incorrectly called innocent. (false negative).

Notice that the test has called 1800 guilty. 900 of them really are guilty BUT the other 900 are not.

So "…what are the odds that you are guilty if the test says you are…?"

Only 50%!!

This may come as a surprise to most people given that the test is 90% accurate, but the result comes as a consequence of the actual guilty rate being only 10% and the error rate of the test being 10%

If the test accuracy is increased to 99% the numbers change to:

9,000 innocent people → 8910 innocent and 90 people incorrectly called guilty

1,000 guilty people -→ 990 guilty and 10 incorrectly called innocent

The test then is calling 90 + 990 = 1080 people guilty of which about 92% really are.

In this case the test is really is trustworthy.

To achieve this the error rate, 1%, has to be 10x lower than the guilty rate of 10%.

In real life we don't actually know the guilty rate. But when it comes to lying, taking drugs in most large corporations or government agencies with educated salaried people, I think it's a pretty safe assumption that the rate is relatively low.

This implies that drug tests as well as lie detector tests are inherently unreliable just based on the statistics alone let alone the actual mechanism of the tests themselves. And in the case of a polygraph it is REALLY suspect.

Now one way around this would be to re-test all the people the tests called guilty.

In our first case we had 900 innocent people called guilty and 900 really guilty people called such.

If we re-test those same 1800 people again the numbers are (at the same 90% accuracy):

- 900 innocent people → 810 called innocent correctly, 90 called guilty incorrectly
- 900 guilty people → 810 correctly called guilty, 90 called innocent incorrectly

The test has identified 90 + 810 = 900 people as guilty and in actuality 90% really ARE guilty.

This is much more trustworthy than a one test and make a decision scenario which is downright scary when you think that one's job and livelihood can swing on the results.

It so happens that most drug testing companies do indeed do this. They always re-test positive samples in order to avoid this type of error.

Polygraph test do so as well usually although the polygraph itself is still flawed based on its inherent assumptions and subjectivity.

As well as the fact it has been established that there are people who can "beat" a polygraph tests. From sociopaths to well-trained Intel assets.

Aldridge Ames, notorious CIA spy and traitor was able to pass 2 polygraph tests in his 15 yr. CIA career of which 10 years he was turning over secrets to the Soviet Union resulting in the executions of many American assets in Russia.

In my old neighborhood of Fredericksburg, VA lived a career FBI person whose job it was to teach field agents working in other countries how not to be followed while living abroad. He also was turning over secrets to the Russians as well and had passed many polygraphs over the years. Turns out in a case of irony, that he himself was followed by FBI investigators for 8 months prior to his arrest and this was totally unbeknownst to him.

So much for expert teaching.

Bottom line, HR personnel must be very careful when using drug or polygraph testing.

SCENARIO 3: Racism, sexism, Ageism oh my!! Bane of HR

MAN VS. THE COLLECTIVE

"Excellence is the best deterrent

to racism or sexism"

Oprah Winfrey

Perhaps nothing is more worrisome and problematic for an HR professional than to deal with issues of racism, sexism, ageism or any "ism".

These "isms " are the worse kind of arguments in a group of people and are absolutely poisonous to any organization.

From massive law suits which can be financially crippling to the mere fact that a loss of reputation and damage to a brand name can totally undermine an otherwise successful and growing company.

Can you imagine trying to recover in this day in age when the consumers of the market place believe your company to be racist or condone racism?

Once that is out there it is hard to win back the trust.

Putting aside the historic and cultural source of racism, sexism and homophobia (as well as religious objections) where does such prejudice come from in today's world? Surely in the year 2014 old time ugly views of people from other groups that one may or may not have met, wouldn't dominate in our culture as it once did in our country's past?

The problem, in many ways, is a statistical one. It is a case of an Ecological fallacy. This is a type of logical fallacy where one errors in the interpretation of statistical data. Where ones inferences about the nature of individuals are deduced from the group to which those individuals belong.

For example:

-since African Americans dominate the cornerback position in the NFL where speed is a premium, therefore all African Americans or at least the average African American must be faster than other ethnic groups.

-since Asian Americans are over represented in engineering classes in universities around the U.S. where math skills are at a premium, therefore the all Asian Americans or at least the average Asian American is better at math than other ethnic groups.

You can make the same observations about women in HR, men in accounting, white males in engineering departments, and on and on.

But what is wrong with this reasoning? Isn't it valid to conclude that the average person in group A or B is superior to other groups if more people from said group end up in certain fields or categories?

On a superficial level this seems cogent.

However let's analyze this a little more closely and deeply.

To start, recall the Bell or Normal curve of statistics. The very think which gives Six Sigma its name.

Let's start with an area that is heavily measured and quantified and where it is believed meritocracy truly carries the day: sports. Specifically let's examine the 40 yard dash times of college cornerbacks.

Some background:

-a corner back in football is usually a smaller player that guards a wide receiver and tries to prevent him from catching the ball when it is passed by the quarterback.

-as a result a corner back needs to be very fast. In fact one of the fastest player on the field.

-it is a fact that in the NFL, African Americans make up nearly 80-90% of all Cornerbacks (CB) in pro football.

-Since African Americans make up such a high percentage of a position that requires speed at the highest level, -→ isn't it then logical that we can conclude that African Americans are on average faster than white and other players?

Below is a snapshot of part of the data taken from Division I, II, III and all levels of college football for corner backs in the U.S. in 2012.

White college CB	Black college CB
5.27	4.31
5.43	4.99
5.19	5.12
4.96	4.30
3.57	5.84
5.64	3.45
4.91	4.73
5.31	3.10
4.90	4.91
4.77	5.86
5.16	4.30
4.61	3.82
5.48	3.84
5.38	5.01
4.93	5.23
5.08	4.07
5.96	4.85
5.40	5.55
4.96	5.39
4.66	6.19
4.99	4.03
5.31	5.32
4.57	5.84
4.76	5.51
5.09	5.30

There are 120 African American CB's and over 700 white CB's measured in this data.

Since there are more white Americans (72% of the US) than African Americans (12%) as well as way more white Americans in college than African Americans, it shouldn't be surprising that there are more white college football players, even CB's than African Americans (Remember we are counting each level of college from NAIA, Division III-players the general public would have never heard of; all the way to the stars of Division I that nearly everyone who is a football fan may know).

Below is a graph of the distribution of the two data sets on the same axis

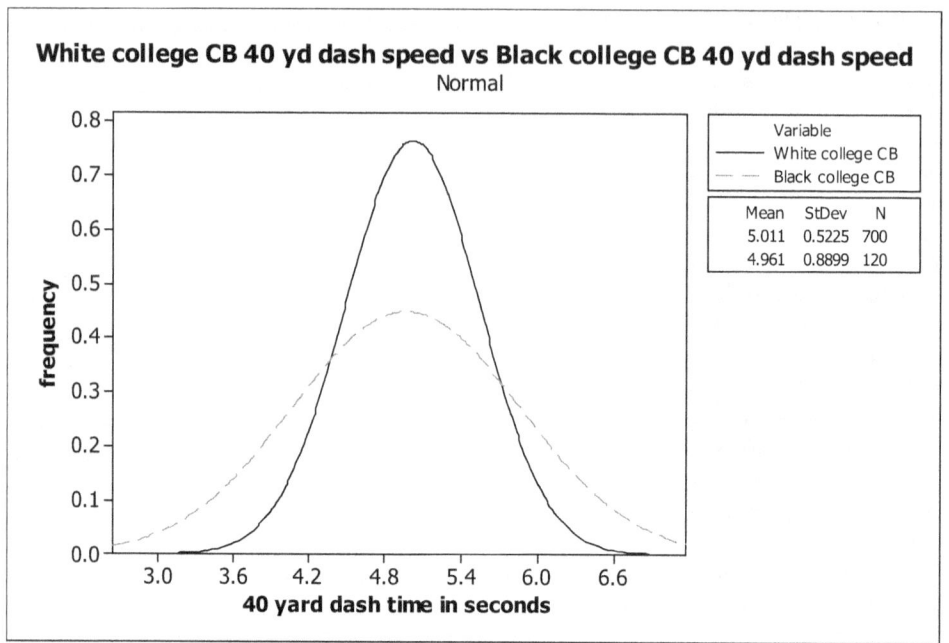

It helps to realize that 4.2 is considered incredibly fast and a speed few humans can achieve.

Now notice this:

-the average, or mean, of the two distributions shows no statistically significant difference between the two.

Minitab analysis reveals:

Two-Sample T-Test and CI: White college CB, Black college CB

Two-sample T for White college CB vs Black college CB

	N	Mean	StDev	SE Mean
White college CB	700	5.011	0.522	0.020
Black college CB	120	4.961	0.890	0.081

Difference = mu (White college CB) - mu (Black college CB)

Estimate for difference: 0.0499

95% CI for difference: (-0.1155, 0.2153)

T-Test of difference = 0 (vs not =): T-Value = 0.60 **P-Value = 0.552**
DF = 133

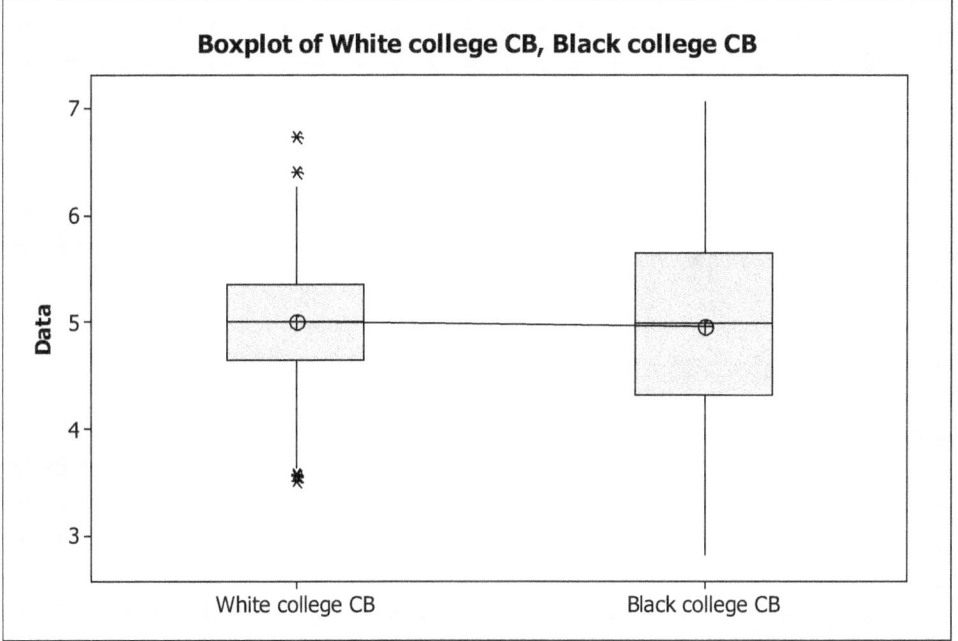

Likewise there is no statistical difference in the MEDIANS of the two groups

Recall that the "median" is the point where 50% of the data is above and 50% of the data is below. Unlike "mean" which is the sum of all the data divided by the number of data points. Or the average

Mann-Whitney Test and CI: White college CB, Black college CB

                N   Median

```
White college CB    700    5.0069
Black college CB    120    4.9868
```

```
Point estimate for ETA1-ETA2 is 0.0375

95.0 Percent CI for ETA1-ETA2 is (-0.1187,0.1902)

W = 288459.0

Test of ETA1 = ETA2 vs ETA1 not = ETA2 is significant at  0.6438

The test is significant at 0.6438 (adjusted for ties)
```

So this answers the question "is the average African American player faster than the average white player".

By this data the answer is, statistically speaking, NO!

But wait---why then are so many of the NFL CB's African American?

Well consider this fact---to be a CB in the NFL you just don't have to be fast; you have to be VERY FAST.

That is faster than nearly anyone else.

If you examine the 40 yard dash times from CB's in the NFL Combine (when the NFL invites over 350 college players to come to Indianapolis and undergo a series of tests prior to any team making a decision to draft them) you find that to be drafted as a CB in the NFL your 40 yard dash speed needs to be:

4.4 or lower (no CB drafted in the NFL over the past 10 years has had a lower 40-yard dash time than this).

The fastest of the fast

Let's re-look at the histograms of the data previously and this time put in the reference point of 4.4 to see how many African American and white CB's fall under that meaning that they are fast enough to play CB in the NFL

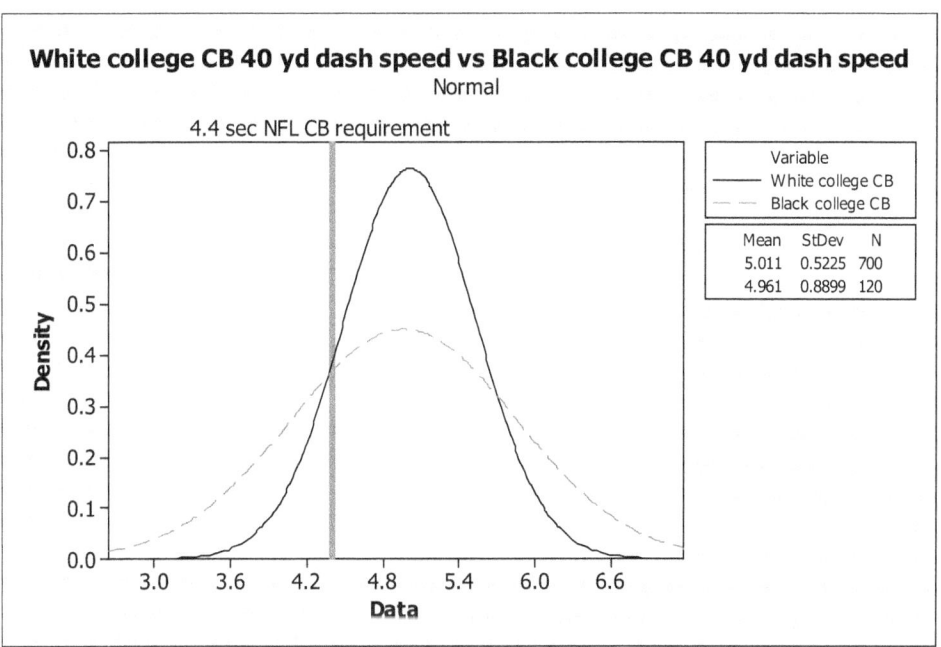

Notice the dotted red line which represents the Black college CB times that are to the LEFT of the line.

Notice also the black line that represents the White college CB times that are also to the LEFT of the 4.4 reference line.

It should be easy to discern that there are indeed a lot more Black college CB times to the left of the line than there are White college CB times. This implies that you would expect a higher percentage of NFL CB's (players with a faster 40 yard dash time than 4.4 or to the left of the line) who are African American than are white even though the average and median of both groups are statistically the same.

In fact we can calculate the exact percentage by using the Six Sigma tool Process Capability Chart on each histogram

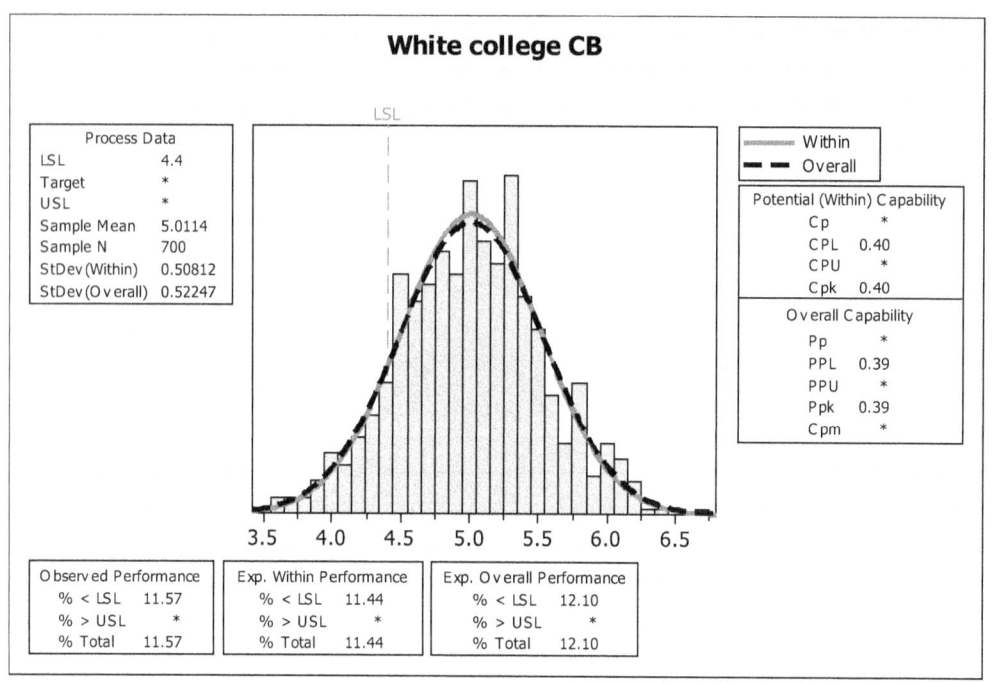

12.1% of the white college CB's meet the standard of 4.4 sec. forty yard dash speed.

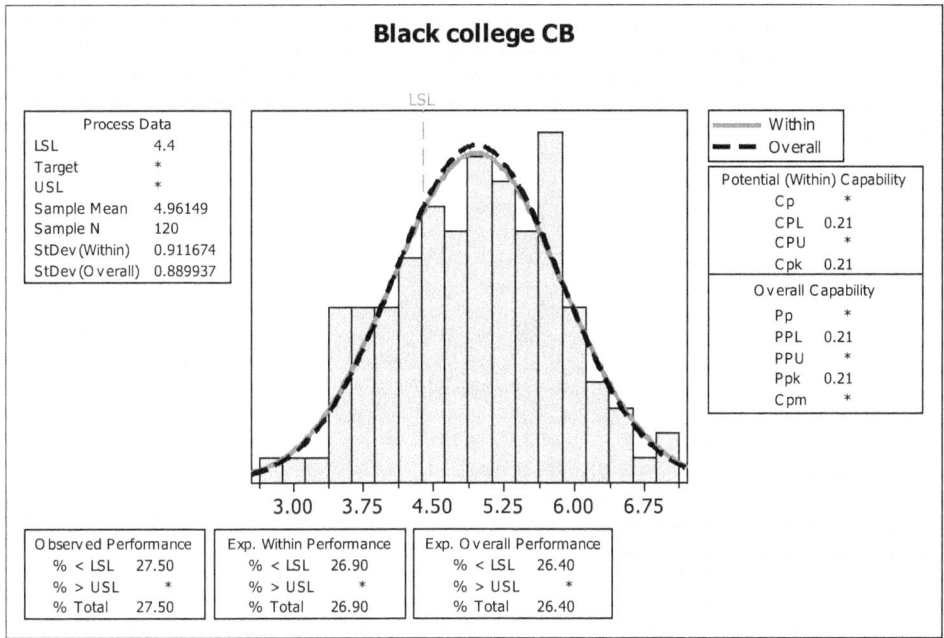

26.4% of African American college CB's meet the standard.

Over twice that of the white college CB's. And when you throw in other required tools such as requiring an even faster 40 speed (4.3 or 4.2 or lower), actually guarding a receiver, football IQ, experience, quickness, etc. it is no wonder African Americans are over represented at the CB position in the NFL

But what happened? How did we go from statistically showing that the average (as well as the median) was not different between the two groups -→ YET at the high performing end one group is way over represented in the jobs where speed is so valued?

This has nothing to do with race, racism or social-cultural bias of any kind.

It is purely a statistical phenomenon.

In this case we were looking at football CB 40 yard dash speeds, but the same thing happens if we look at

-SAT scores.

-IQ tests.

Or any type of tests where we are trying to find the best (or worse) of some type of measurement.

Also the same thing could exist if the means and/or medians were slightly different yet the variances differed as they did here.

The odds of any two groups having exactly the same metrics in terms of mean, median, standard deviation, skew, is probably small. But just because there is a slight difference in any of these doesn't imply that on balance there is a real meaningful difference between said groups.

In fact "race" itself is no longer considered a biological classification of human beings and hasn't been held such by scientist in over 40 years.

The reason being is that the difference WITHIN a given racial group is greater than the difference BETWEEN other racial groups.

What I mean by this is that the difference between African Americans at each end of the spectrum is far more severe than the difference BETWEEN the average African American and average White American.

Likewise the difference between one side of people who classify themselves as white and the other end of that same classification, is greater than the difference between the average White American and average African American.

The Six Sigma tool which analyzes groups of data to determine if real statistically significant difference exists between "means" based on the differences "within" said groups is ANOVA. Or Analysis of Variance.

What an ANOVA can basically tell you is that if the variation in the data within 2 or more groups of data sets is too great then that will over shadow any difference that you could possibly see between the mean or average of those same groups of data.

Below is a graph that shows exactly what I am attempting to express. Notice that the variation is so great for each group that there is no way to see any difference in the means/averages.

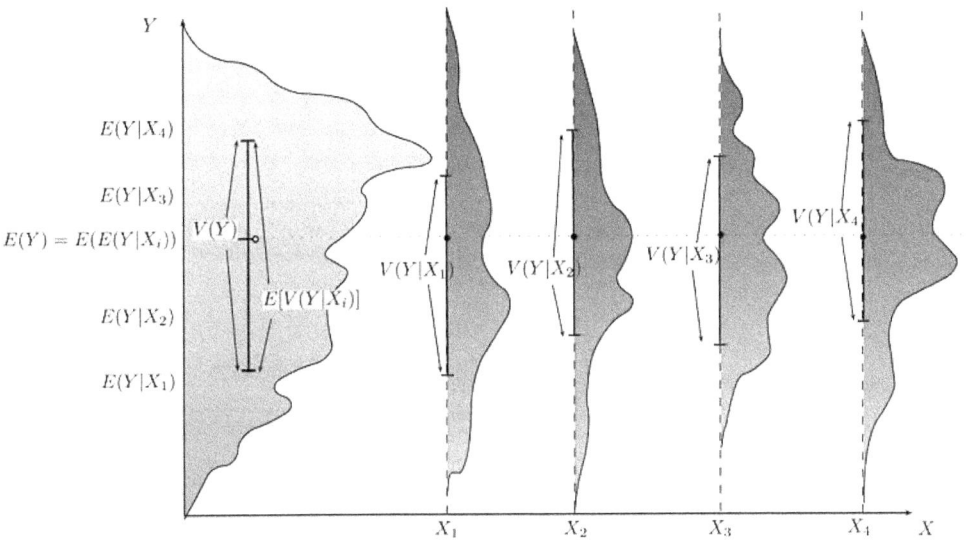

Figure 2: ANOVA : No fit

Now here is a graph there the variation is small enough that a difference between the mean/averages can be adequately discerned.

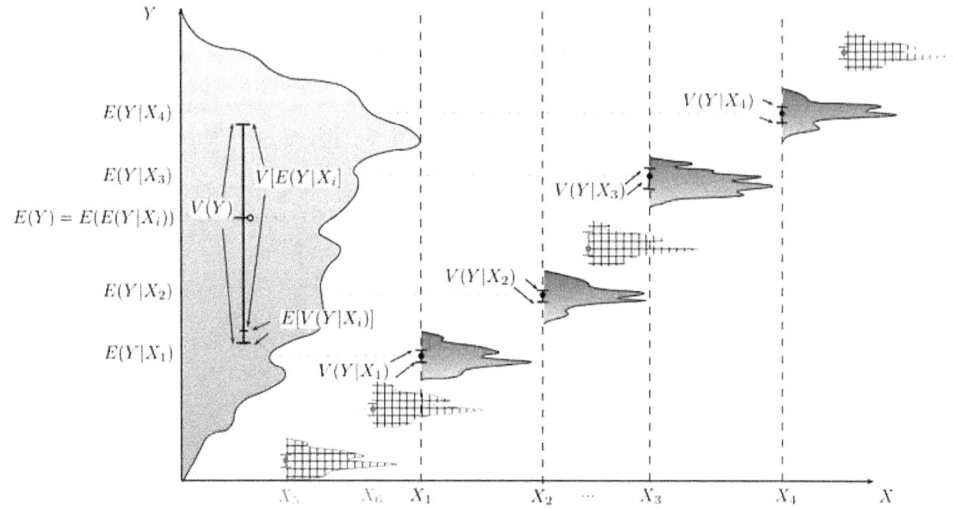

Figure 3: ANOVA : very good fit

On a final note: "race" while no longer a biological scientifically meaningful term, still does have validity in that it is a CULTURAL classification.

Clearly there are differences in the cultures of people of different races in countries like the U.S.

Race is determine (if that is a fair word) by only one way in the U.S.—self classification.

The only way the US government knows there are 12% African Americans, 13% Hispanic, 72% white, etc. is due to the self-classification of the citizens in census forms and polls.

Barrack Obama himself who is of mixed-race due to having a white mother and black father, classifies himself as black probably because he basically LOOKS black and is viewed by others as being black.

Same for Tiger Woods.

Bottom line is that race is not biological but cultural and is totally self-defined.

(Note: for what it is worth President Obama is not Muslim either. He only met his father twice in his life that he recalled and his father, while being Kenyan a predominately Muslim country, was an avowed atheist and not a practicing Muslim who would not have attempted to raise his son in that religion even had he been in his life growing up).

Tests that attempt to find people at the extremes of performance in areas such as speed, test scores, intelligence (supposedly. We ignore the socio-economic and cultural issues of something like an IQ test in this analysis. That is a whole other issue) may indeed filter out a higher proportion of people of one race or another BUT that this does not statistically imply that the average person from either of the races are different from one another.

This is yet another situation that can be controversial and awkward where Six Sigma statistical tools can come to the aid of the HR professional.

Scenario 4: Only the good get ahead. Or the lucky…

MAN VS. CHANCE

> "A man sees what he wants to see and
> Disregards the rest…"
>
> "The Boxer" Simon and Garfunkel

If you work hard you will be successful.

All success is basically, is hard dedicated work.

This ethos is ripe in corporate America and in fact is fully ingrained in the American psyche through and through. It's part of our core. Our DNA so to speak.

But is it true?

Are the people who are successful really so just due to hard work?

While it's true that successful people do work hard.

But don't a lot of UNSUCCESSFUL people work hard also?

Ever seen a ditch digger, a roofer, or millions and millions of America's poor that do back braking work for sometimes up to 16 hrs. a day?

Aren't they working hard?

In fact most of America's working poor have 2 sometimes 3 jobs yet no one would say they are successful.

(Note: in this context we mean "successful" to be financially so. So spiritual, mental fulfillment while clearly important and perhaps MORE important isn't rolling up in this particular analysis we will do here.)

If hard work is what brings success then why isn't everyone who works several jobs 14-16 hrs. per day doing very well financially?

It is a fact that people who start their own businesses are some of the hardest working people in our country. Yet 85% of new businesses fail financially within the first 5 years. If you look out to 10 years that number grows to 95%.

This is sort of like evolution applied to economics in a sense.

Aren't those people working hard? Surely we don't believe that all those businesses are failing due to lack of hard work of so many business founders?

We can't say that America is a hard working country on one hand, yet have so many non-hard working people in it, on the other. Especially when you consider that we have had a 15-17% poverty rate since the late 1960's.

The point here is that working hard maybe NECESSARY, it is not **SUFFICIENT** to be successful.

You can work very hard at a bad idea and guess what-you won't be around long in business.

You can work very hard and even have a successful business, say like selling a new fashion line of clothes and in a year or two the fashion taste changes and all of a sudden you have a load of inventory you can't move and now you are in trouble. Not because you got lazy and quit working hard. But because the market changed and product of your hard work while once valued, now no long is through no fault of your own.

The list of bankrupt companies run by hard working me in just that type of scenario far outnumber the list of successful companies in history.

So why bring up this point in a book discussing Six Sigma Tools applied to HR?

I think it is important to a HR professional when they look at the people in their organization, that being successful doesn't necessarily mean that a person is the hardest working or even the most talented.

Consider this scenario:

Say there are 1,000 very talented engineers in an organization and each of them are given a project and for this example let's assume that the projects are of equal importance to the company and of equal difficulty in being successful.

Let's also assume that there is a 50-50 chance that a project will be successful for each engineer.

The company is going to give a bonus and a promotion for each engineer who has a successful project. Furthermore each of the successful engineers will be given a 2nd project and the same assumptions for this project also applies.

Since we have

- 1,000 engineers each with a project

- 50-50 chance of a project being successful for each of engineer.

Then 500 engineers will be successful and 500 will not be.

Those 500 that are successful get a bonus, a promotion and a 2nd project.

So now we have

-500 engineers each given an additional project

- 50-50 chance of each project being successful

Then again we will have 250 engineers who will get a bonus, a promotion and now a 3rd project.

With the 3rd project we have 250 with a 50-50 chance of having a successful project which will leave 125 engineers at the end of the process with a bonus and promotion.

If we play this out for 7 projects you can see something like this

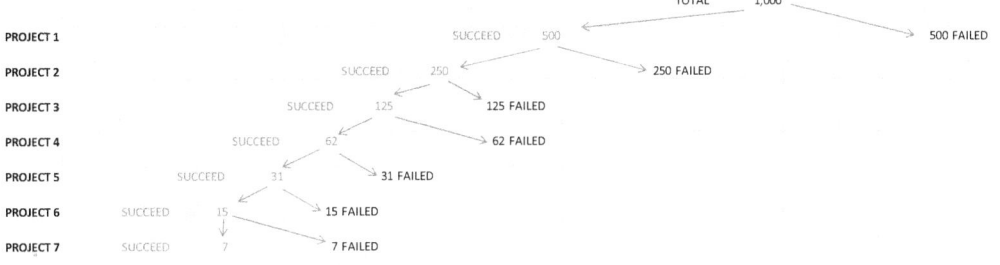

After 7 projects we have 7 people who have completed all of them successfully.

Now the natural inclination of the HR people and in fact everyone in the company is that these must be the most talented, hardest working, get it done types in the whole company. And guess what? They get promoted and these are the future leaders who have the highest positions in most corporations and make future decisions including the decisions on who in the future will be considered for later promotions and bonuses.

But is this view warranted?

Notice that in this case it was ALL LUCK!

The 7 people who completed all 7 projects successfully in this scenario were no different than any of the other engineers.

Yet from the outside it LOOKS or appears that they must be the most successful and hardest working engineers since they never failed once in 7 tries.

The odds of doing 7 projects with each having a 50-50 chance of failing, and having them all successful is only

2^7 =128

Or once chance out of 1/128 which is .78%

Very small.

It's easy to see how an outside observer may see this and say "hey those people MUST be the best and the brightest since the odds of them doing all 7 projects successfully is so small".

But this is very short sighted.

Many of you may recognize this as a common stock market mail scam. What happens is that a con artist will send out letters to 1,000 people. 500 of them he will say that Stock A will go up this week. The other 500 he will say Stock A will go down this week.

Notice that half the people will see him as being correct.

He can do this for 7 straight weeks by only sending later letters to the previous people he sent to that saw a correct prediction. And the people in the end will think he must have some powerful stock picking powers and send him their money to invest in his skills.

He doesn't of course. It's just a scam. .

Many times people in HR, corporate America and America in general misconstrue luck for innate skill in the person on the receiving end.

Bestselling author Malcolm Gladwell wrote a book "Outliers" that went into detail on this type of phenomenon. (A fantastic read by the way if you haven't already read it).

The point of all this is that HR professionals need to be careful and consider a bigger picture when they evaluate talent and determine who are "hi-pots" (high potential employees deserving of a special look when considering promotions) in any given organization.

What may look like the product of hard work and skill often times can just be the manifestation of luck and simple statistics.

SUMMARY

Traditionally Human Resources has been viewed as a liberal arts, soft skill, "touchy-feely" type of professional. Meanwhile a methodology like Six Sigma is often viewed as a hard, technical, mathematical and technical type of method that is most suited for manufacturing and engineering.

All the above is true to a large extent.

But so what of it?

The tools of Six Sigma can be employed in any field.

The "people", intuitive skills of Human Resources can use any technical method to its advantage while not losing the essence of what makes it so unique among career paths.

Six Sigma has been used in such diverse areas as making good wine, art auctions, music recording, and other non-technical type of areas far removed from the hard science arena of manufacturing and engineering.

Likewise HR, is used in the NFL, boxing and UFC and the military. Finding, vetting, training, grooming, developing and even getting rid of certain people in certain jobs is something that is universal in any field.

After reading this book I think you can now see how understanding and using the tools of Six Sigma can be a big win for any Human Resource professional regardless of the industry they happen to work in.

I personally have seen it first hand and have heard or read it about it thousands of more times second hand.

A HR person need not be a statistician (no one excelling in Six Sigma need be in fact) fully engage Six Sigma. As long as someone can understand a problem, frame it in a quantifiable manner, know how to gather trustworthy data, how to analyze it, how to make changes, see improvements and hold those improvements in place over time-then that is Six Sigma in a nutshell.

That is DMAIC

Define

Measure

Improve

And finally

Control.

The Six Sigma DMAIC method is just human reasoning which man has mastered over the millennium given a new more rigorous and formal face-lift.

And who can say good reasoning is every out of vogue?

THE END

www.ingramcontent.com/pod-product-compliance
Lightning Source LLC
˜mbersburg PA
˜71759170526
7CB00003B/1092